WARS AT HOME
America Forms an Identity (1812-1820)

TITLE LIST

WARS AT HOME
America Forms an Identity (1812-1820)

BY MICHELLE QUINBY

MASON CREST

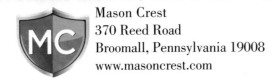

Mason Crest
370 Reed Road
Broomall, Pennsylvania 19008
www.masoncrest.com

Printed and bound in Hashemite Kingdom of Jordan.

First printing
9 8 7 6 5 4 3 2 1

Library of Congress Cataloging-in-Publication Data

Quinby, Michelle.
  Wars at home : America forms an identity (1812-1820) / Michelle Quinby.
     p. cm.
  Includes bibliographical references and index.
   ISBN 978-1-4222-2401-4 (hardcover) — ISBN 978-1-4222-2396-3 (hardcover series) ISBN 978-1-4222-9311-9 (ebook)
  1. United States—History—1809-1817—Juvenile literature. 2. United States—History—1817-1825—Juvenile literature. 3. United States—History—War of 1812—Juvenile literature. 4. Nationalism—United States—History—19th century. 5. National characteristics, American—History—19th century—Juvenile literature. 6. Florida—History—Cession to the United States, 1819—Juvenile literature. I. Title.
  E341.Q56 2012
  973.5—dc22
                                    2011000840

Produced by Harding House Publishing Services, Inc.
www.hardinghousepages.com
Cover design by Torque Advertising + Design.

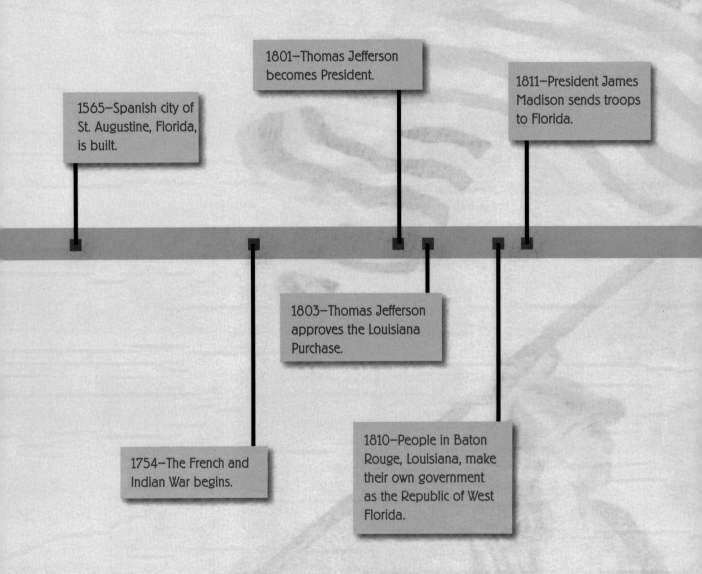

1801–Thomas Jefferson becomes President.

1811–President James Madison sends troops to Florida.

1565–Spanish city of St. Augustine, Florida, is built.

1803–Thomas Jefferson approves the Louisiana Purchase.

1754–The French and Indian War begins.

1810–People in Baton Rouge, Louisiana, make their own government as the Republic of West Florida.

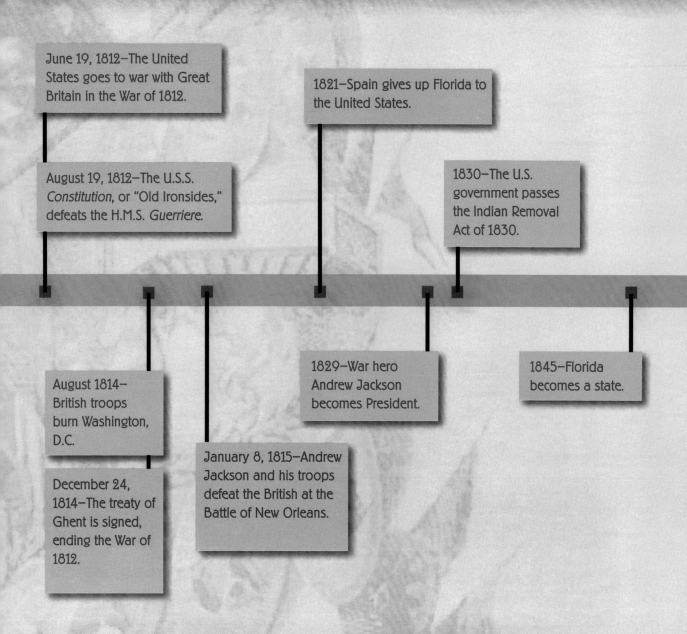

June 19, 1812–The United States goes to war with Great Britain in the War of 1812.

1821–Spain gives up Florida to the United States.

August 19, 1812–The U.S.S. *Constitution*, or "Old Ironsides," defeats the H.M.S. *Guerriere*.

1830–The U.S. government passes the Indian Removal Act of 1830.

August 1814– British troops burn Washington, D.C.

1829–War hero Andrew Jackson becomes President.

1845–Florida becomes a state.

December 24, 1814–The treaty of Ghent is signed, ending the War of 1812.

January 8, 1815–Andrew Jackson and his troops defeat the British at the Battle of New Orleans.

Chapter One
AMERICANS GROW PROUD

The people who lived in the United States were proud of their new country. But most of them didn't really think of themselves as Americans. Being an American wasn't that important to them. They didn't have a sense of nationalism. They needed to start thinking of themselves as Americans. They had to believe America was a great place. They needed to be willing to work hard to build their country. If the United States was going to be strong, Americans had to believe it could last. They had to be sure of their country's future.

Some things helped pull Americans together. They had a lot in common. They had made themselves new lives in North America. They loved freedom. They believed all people should be equal. (All white men, anyway. It would take quite a bit longer before

Nationalism is the feeling that you belong to a nation, a country. It means you feel pride in your country. You may believe your country is better than other countries. Being a part of your country is an important part of how you think about yourself.

women and people of other races were thought of as equals!) They were hard-working people. They were brave. They shared a lot of beliefs, too. Most of them were Christians.

At first, though, Americans didn't want to have anything to do with the rest of the world's business. George Washington, the first President of the United States, didn't want Americans to get pulled into foreign wars. European countries like Britain and France were often at war. Washington worried that the United States wasn't strong enough to handle a war. Americans needed to pay attention to their own country first.

By the time Thomas Jefferson, the third President, left office in 1809, Europe was a tense place. Like America, France had gone through a **revolution**. Now, Napoleon Bonaparte, France's leader, wanted to take over the world. The French were excited about their country. Britain was worried, though. Britain didn't want France becoming too strong. So Britain went to war with France.

The United States didn't wanted to take sides in the war. Americans didn't want to get pulled into the fight between France and Britain. But the French and British didn't let the United States stay out of it. They didn't think of the United States as a "real" country. They captured American ships and forced American sailors to work for them. Americans were really, really mad!

The way Britain and France treated the United States made the people in the United States draw closer together more than they had before. They started to think of themselves as Americans. Their sense of nationalism was growing.

Thomas Jefferson tried to force Britain and France to respect the United States. He stopped all **trade** with those countries until they promised to leave the United States

A **revolution** is when the people in a country fight together to change their government.

Trade is the exchange of goods between countries.

British impressment of U.S. soldiers

Columbia TEACHING John Bull his new LESSON

Political cartoon describing British invasion of America's rights on the seas

alone. He wanted them to agree that the United States could be **neutral** in the European war. James Madison, who was President after Jefferson, tried the same thing.

Someone who is **neutral** doesn't take sides in a war or an argument.

Stopping foreign trade didn't work, though. Americans needed goods from France and Britain. They needed supplies for their factories. American businesses ended up being hurt more than European businesses. Americans started smuggling goods down through Canada to get what they needed.

In 1810, Congress passed a law that the Unites States could trade with European countries again. The law also said that if either France or Britain agreed to respect

James Madison

Henry Clay

America's right to stay out of the war, the United States would stop trade with the other country. Immediately, Napoleon said France would respect America's neutrality. So President Madison stopped trade with Britain again.

Meanwhile, Britain was also moving in on America's Western territory. This made Americans even angrier. It was like Britain was saying they weren't a real country.

Americans disagreed about what they should do. Older people, who remembered the Revolutionary War, didn't want another war. They knew how bad war could be. The younger leaders, though, like Henry Clay and Andrew Jackson, pushed for war. They wanted to teach Britain a lesson. They thought Americans should prove to Britain how strong they were. People called them the War Hawks, because they really wanted to fight.

General Andrew Jackson

The British finally promised to stop capturing American sailors. It was too late, though. Americans were mad at the British for trying to take land in the West. The British were banding together with the Native tribes. This scared many Americans.

The War Hawks had had enough. They persuaded Congress to start a war. In June of 1812, the United States went to war against Britain. This became known as the War of 1812.

TECUMSEH, AN IMPORTANT NATIVE LEADER

Tecumseh's real name, his Native name, was Tekamthi. He was born on March 9, 1768, as a shooting star streaked across the night sky. His father, a Shawnee chief, knew this was a great sign.

As he grew up, Tekamthi saw how the white men were moving west. The white settlers were pushing the Native tribes off the land. Tekamthi wanted to find a way to live peacefully with the white men. But he always wanted to make sure his people did not lose their homes.

He knew if the tribes stood together, they would be too strong for the white men to defeat. He said that a Native tribe by itself was like a single hair. The white men could easily snap it. But together, the tribes would be like a braid. They would be too strong to be broken.

Drawing of Tecumseh by Benson Lossing

Tekamthi traveled across North America. He brought his message to all the Native tribes. His brother, a religious leader, went with him. People called them Tecumseh and the Prophet.

Before Tekamthi could pull the tribes together, though, the Americans stopped them. The American army destroyed an entire Native village. Native people were scared. They no longer believed Takamthi's message.

Instead, Tekamthi turned to the British for help. After all, they had the same goal. They both wanted to keep the United States from expanding.

Tekamthi (actual likeness)   The Prophet

Chapter Two
THE WAR OF 1812

The United States wasn't really ready for a war. The American army had only 12,000 soldiers. Most of the officers didn't have any experience. Many Americans didn't want the war. They thought it was a terrible idea. Other Americans, though, wanted to teach Britain a lesson. They wanted to prove that the United States couldn't be pushed around.

Canada was the United States' closest neighbor. It wasn't a country yet, though. It still belonged to Britain. The Americans knew they could best attack Britain in Canada. One group of American soldiers went through Detroit, Michigan. Another crossed the Niagara River to attack. The third crossed Lake Champlain and moved toward Montreal.

The Americans thought they wouldn't have any trouble invading Canada. Americans believed that the people living in Canada would be glad to be freed from Britain. They thought Canadians would want to join the United States. So the army expected the Canadians to turn against the British and help them.

But that's not what happened! Instead, the Americans lost badly. The British captured the city of Detroit. The troops who had crossed the Niagara River were quickly defeated. Those who had gone toward Montreal refused to fight.

The war was not only fought in Canada, though. The British had the best navy in the world. They brought more than a thousand ships to block U.S. ports. They didn't want the Americans to be able to get in or out. They didn't want them to be able to do business with other countries. The Americans had only fourteen ships. The fight didn't look very fair. The British seemed likely to win at sea, as well.

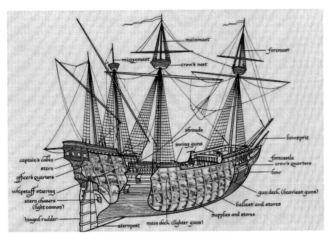

When the American ships fought the British in battle, though, they did very well. In one sea battle, the British shot their cannons at the U.S.S. *Constitution*. The cannonballs bounced off the ship's sides! "Her sides are made of iron!" shouted an American sailor. Really, the ship was made of live oak, the hardest wood in the world. The **hull** was two feet thick. No wonder the cannonballs bounced off!

Americans were proud. They began calling the *Constitution* "Old Ironsides." The ship became a symbol of pride and hope.

The war started to drag on. Mostly, the British were able to keep the Americans from using their seaports. Businessmen had a hard time getting the goods they needed. American businesses had a hard time.

The Americans weren't able to invade Canada—but the British weren't able to defeat the Americans completely, either. Meanwhile, in the West, American general William

A ship's **hull** is its main body or frame.

The U.S.S. *Constitution*, "Old Ironsides"

Henry Harrison was building an army. On the Great Lakes, naval officer Oliver Hazard Perry put together an inland navy.

On September 10, 1813, Perry led the Battle of Lake Erie. The battle was a huge victory for the Americans. They captured all the British ships. This meant the British had no way to get supplies to

Oliver Hazard Perry at the Battle of Lake Erie in 1813

their troops in the West anymore. Then William Henry Harrison pushed in from the West with his army. The British left Detroit. They went back into Canada. Things were looking good for the Americans.

Up until now, the British had also been fighting a war with Napoleon in Europe. They hadn't been able to give all their attention to the war in North America. Then, in 1814, the British and their **allies** beat Napoleon. Now, Britain had more soldiers and weapons they could use in their war with the United States.

The British attacked the United States in three places. They sent troops down through Lake Champlain and along the Hudson River. They wanted to cut off New England from the rest of the United States. They also attacked New Orleans, in order to block the Mississippi River. The Mississippi River was very important to American trade. American plantations in the South shipped their goods on the river to factories in the North. The factories in the North sailed their goods back down the river to the South. Without the river, American businesses would be in even bigger trouble. The third place the British attacked was the Chesapeake Bay. The British wanted to pull American troops away from the other two battles. The British wanted to beat the Americans quickly. They wanted to end the war.

For a while, things looked very bad for the Americans. The British drove in through the Chesapeake Bay. Then they marched on Washington, D.C. When they reached the city, they burned as many government buildings as they could. The Capitol and the President's mansion were both badly damaged.

Allies are countries (or people) who have agreed to fight on the same side against each other's enemies.

THE WHITE HOUSE

After the British burned the President's mansion, its walls were black with smoke. People painted it with white paint to cover the burn marks. Now the mansion was a gleaming white! And that's how it got its nickname—"The White House."

Then, on September 11, 1814, the American navy destroyed the British fleet on Lake Champlain. The British pulled back. They didn't want to lose more troops.

Meanwhile, in Europe, in the city of Ghent, men from both sides were trying to work out an agreement. They wanted to end the war without any more fighting. They were trying to find a peaceful answer that would make everyone happy. With the British defeat on Lake Champlain, the Americans had more power to bargain for the things they wanted.

Everyone was very tired of war. On December 24, 1814, the Americans and the British signed the Treaty of Ghent. The War of 1812 was over.

News took a long time to cross the Atlantic Ocean, though. General Andrew Jackson was leading the American forces in the South. He did not know the war was over. He marched first on Pensacola, Florida. Florida was Spanish territory. British and Native American soldiers had gone there to be safe. But Jackson went right ahead and attacked them anyway. He won. Then, Jackson moved on to New Orleans. The British soldiers

Signing of the Treaty of Ghent

Battle of New Orleans

there outnumbered the Americans by more than two to one. Jackson went ahead and beat them anyway!

Nobody really won the War of 1812. The British won some battles. The Americans won others. When it was over, things mostly went back to the way they had been before. The way Americans thought about themselves had changed, though. They had survived another war, their first as an independent country.

The Battle of New Orleans turned out to be one of the most important battles of the war. The Americans felt proud whenever they thought of how they had won against such bad odds. Andrew Jackson became an American hero.

Now, more than ever, Americans wanted to make their country bigger. They had mostly given up on spreading into Canada—but they still wanted to move West. And taking over Florida, too, seemed like the next step.

GEORGIA

former boundary of West Florida

Claim of Spain relinquished in 1795

Wakefield Ft. Stoddert

MISSISSIPPI TERRITORY

Organized in 1798

Mobile Ft. St.

Baton
Rouge

Natchez

WEST FLORIDA EAST

Baton
Rouge

New Orleans

Pensacola

Apalachee Bay

St. Marks

FLORIDA

St. Augustine

Savannah

GULF OF MEXICO

e

25

85

Chapter Three
FLORIDA AND THE UNITED STATES

In 1513, the first Europeans arrived in what is now Florida. They were Spanish. A man named Ponce de León led them. He was looking for a fountain that would make people live forever. He never found his fountain of youth. He did, however, begin the European settlement of Florida.

Before the Europeans arrived, hundreds of thousands of Native people lived there. For the next three hundred years, though, the French, the Spanish, and sometimes the English settled Florida. Some Natives died in battles with the Europeans. But thousands and thousands more died from diseases that the Europeans brought with them. Some villages or tribes were completely wiped out.

Generally, the Spanish had a friendly relationship with the Native people, though. They did not treat them as equals—but they did not treat them as badly as many of the English settlers did. The Spanish in Florida bought and sold both Africans and Natives as slaves. But the Spanish saw slavery differently from the way the English did. Spanish slaves earned money. They were able to use their money to buy their own houses. They were also able to buy their own freedom. They didn't have to be slaves forever.

Many Native people died because of the Spanish.

The Spanish worried about the English colonies north of Florida. They were afraid the English would push them out of Florida. They wanted to make their colony stronger. In 1693, the Spanish offered freedom to any English slaves who went to Florida. They also welcomed Natives who wanted to move into Florida and settle. They hoped that

A reconstruction of the interior and exterior of a Native home

if more people lived in Florida, Florida would be stronger. They hoped the Africans and Natives would help them defend Florida against the English.

The English were unhappy with the Spanish in Florida. They didn't like the Spanish persuading English slaves to escape and head south. The English thought of it as stealing. For years, they launched attacks across the Florida border. They burned towns to the ground. They killed people and captured others.

Then Britain (England) took control of Florida. So when the Revolutionary War came along, Spain sided with the American colonies. Spain wanted Britain to be weaker. During the war, Spain got back part of Florida. The agreement that ended the war gave Spain back the rest.

Spain had sided with the Americans during the Revolutionary War. But now the Spanish were nervous about the new United States. The Spanish could see that the new country wanted more land. The Spanish didn't want to lose Florida again. The people who were most nervous were the Africans and Natives who lived in Florida. They knew they would lose their freedom if the Americans got control of Florida.

The Spanish government worried some of the more wealthy people in Florida might want to join the United States. So the Spanish tried to give people reasons to stay in Florida. They gave businesspeople special privileges for doing business in Florida. They also offered free land to anyone who wanted to settle there. The free land attracted a lot of people.

The outcome was very different from what the Spanish had hoped. They had wanted to make Florida look like a better place to live than the United States. When American settlers flooded across the border for the free land, though, Florida started to look a lot like the United States. The new settlers thought of themselves as Americans. They wanted to make Florida part of the United States.

At that time, Florida was larger than it is today. It stretched all the way to the Mississippi River. In 1810, the people of Baton Rouge set up their own government. They called themselves the Republic of West Florida. They said they were now an independent country.

President James Madison decided the United States should take advantage of the situation. He argued that West Florida was really supposed to belong to the United States. He said the area had actually been part of the Louisiana Purchase. Then, the United States took West Florida.

The next year, in 1811, Congress sent American troops

Museum display of a Seminole warrior

to fight along Florida's border. The attacks had to be a secret. If Spain got upset, Congress wanted to be able to say they didn't know anything about the fighting.

These attacks were mainly against the Seminole people. The name "Seminole" came from a Spanish word meaning "runaway." White settlers had pushed many Native tribes out of Georgia and Alabama a hundred years earlier. These tribes moved into Florida. They became known as the Seminoles, or the Red Seminoles. African slaves also fled into Florida. They were known as the Black Seminoles.

The Seminoles—especially the Black Seminoles—knew they would lose their freedom if the United States took Florida. They fought as hard as they could. If they lost, they were taken to the United States. There they were sold as slaves.

When the War of 1812 broke out, Britain helped the Seminoles fight America. Even after the war ended, though, the fighting in northern

Seminoles hid in Florida's many swamps to escape Jackson's troops.

34

Florida continued. The Seminoles raided towns across the border in the United States. The Americans raided Seminole towns in Florida.

General Andrew Jackson was in charge of the attacks on Florida. He said that the Seminoles were dangerous. He said that Spain was too weak to control them. He used this argument as an excuse for attacking Florida. In 1818, Jackson invaded Florida with a force of 1,800 troops.

But Jackson hadn't gotten permission from Congress to attack Florida. He didn't care. During the spring of 1818, he pushed into Florida. He and his soldiers did a lot of damage. They burned Seminole towns. Jackson arrested and killed two British men. Finally, he captured the city of Pensacola. Then he set himself up as governor of Florida.

President Monroe was mad at Jackson. He worried Jackson might have started another war with Britain and with Spain. He tried to fix the situation by giving Florida back to Spain. This shocked Jackson. The American people weren't happy, either. They thought Jackson was a hero.

Spain was getting tired of having to deal with all the trouble in Florida. They saw now how easily the United States could take over. They agreed to sell Florida to the United States for five million dollars.

General Andrew Jackson was still very popular with the American people. After Spain agreed to sell Florida, Jackson went on a tour around the United States to celebrate. People loved him! Finally, President Monroe gave in. He made Jackson governor of the new Florida territory.

The Seminoles were very upset. They were scared. They knew they could lose all their freedom. Spain had tried to protect them. The **treaty** that gave Florida to the United

A **treaty** is an agreement between two or more countries.

Jackson at Pensacola

States said that everyone in Florida would have full rights and citizenship in the United States. That meant Natives and Africans would have the same rights as the whites who lived there. Many Black Seminoles didn't trust the treaty, though. They didn't trust the United States. Two hundred of them fled Florida. They moved to the Bahamas.

The Black Seminoles were right. One of the first things Andrew Jackson did was cancel the part of the treaty that gave Africans and Natives citizenship. He wasn't happy about any of the Seminoles being there. He wanted the Natives to leave.

Life in Florida became very hard for the Seminoles and Black Seminoles. People who had lived comfortable lives were now left with nothing. Anyone who was married to a black or Native person was also in trouble. Mixed-race people were thought of as

Seminoles. Slave catchers were everywhere. Many blacks fled to Haiti or Cuba. Other Seminoles moved into the wilderness areas to escape.

Andrew Jackson did not last long as governor of Florida. His wife became sick in the Florida climate. He missed his home in Tennessee. He wanted a chance to shape the United States. He was afraid he'd be left out if he stayed in Florida. After less than six months as governor, Jackson quit.

But he had changed the history of Florida forever.

TWO POINTS OF VIEW

Have you ever noticed that two people can see the same person very differently? Maybe you've had a teacher that you really didn't like—but your brother or sister had the same teacher and loved her. Why do you think that was? Was one of you right and the other wrong? Or were you both right? Did you just see different sides of the same person?

Why do you think Americans loved Andrew Jackson so much? How do you think most people in America would have described him? How do you think the Seminoles and Black Seminoles would have described him? Who do you think was right?

Chapter Four
AMERICA'S GROWING PAINS

The United States had been started with a lot of good ideas. The Founding Fathers—the men who had started America—had great thoughts about what they wanted the country to be like. They wanted the country to be free. They wanted it to be able to stand on its own, without any help from other countries. They believed people should have the right to choose their own government. They believed all white men should be equals.

Many Americans also believed the United States had the right to more land. Some people worried about this, though. They thought that if America's borders kept getting bigger, it wouldn't be the kind of country they wanted it to be. A country with more land would need a strong army to protect its land. It would need a strong **central** government. It would need more taxes to pay for the government. People worried that these things would be the beginning of the end for America. They were afraid a government

Something that is **central** is at the center.

like this might start to **oppress** the people. They wanted people to have an equal say, no matter whether they were poor or rich. They were afraid this might not happen if the central government made all the decisions.

Other people worried about America's growth for different reasons. They didn't like how the United States had used force to get more land. Invading other people's land and attacking them didn't seem like a good way to spread **democracy**.

When Andrew Jackson invaded Florida, Americans had different reactions. Lots of people thought he was a hero. Other people didn't like what he had done. They didn't like seeing the United States disrespect other people's lives. That was what Britain had done to them, after all.

Americans also disagree about how the United States should treat Native Americans. In 1829, Andrew Jackson became president of the United States. The next year, he helped pass the Indian Removal Act. This was a law that said all the Native people east of the Mississippi River had to move west, to the other side of the Mississippi River.

Some Native Americans fled further west into the wilderness areas. Others signed treaties that were supposed to give them new land. The U.S. Army marched them a thousand miles to their new land. Many of the marches took place in bad weather. People often did not have warm clothes. They didn't have enough food to eat. Thousands of Natives died. They died of starvation. They died from the cold. And they died from sickness.

Some Americans were glad to see the Natives move west. Whites wanted their land. Even before they left, settlers were moving in and taking over the land.

To **oppress** means to keep people down by using unfair or cruel force.

Democracy is a form of government where the people choose their leaders.

CHEROKEE CHOCTAW MUSCOGEE (CREEK)

CHICKASAW SEMINOLE

Known as the Five Civilized Tribes, these Native American nations were forced to relocate because of the Indian Removal Act.

Other Americans were horrified at the situation, though. People in the Northern United States, especially, were upset at how the Native tribes were being treated. Many saw the Indian Removal Act as a mark of disgrace against the United States. They were upset that the U.S. government was destroying the Native way of life.

Still, Americans wanted the land. And not very many people spoke up for the tribes. The marches went on, moving the Natives west.

American leaders started using the phrase "Manifest Destiny" to describe the settlers moving west. They meant they believed God wanted the United States to get new land. Many Americans started to believe they had a God-given right to move west. They even believed that God wanted them to spread over the land. This way, they said, they would spread democracy. They would also spread Christianity. They would bring the white way of life wherever they settled. This belief let many Americans think they had done the right thing by moving the Native people off their land. It took away their guilt.

WHAT DOES "MANIFEST DESTINY" MEAN?

Something that is "manifest" is obvious. It's something that's so clear you can tell it's true just by glancing at it. "Destiny" means the future is already set in place. It's a course of events that can't be avoided. It's just plain bound to happen. So "Manifest Destiny" meant that Americans believed it was just plain obvious that white settlers should spread across the continent. It meant that there was no point even trying to find another way to act because it was bound to happen. It was clearly God's will! Thinking this way meant Americans didn't have to figure out what was right or wrong. They could take away land from Native people without calling themselves thieves. It made them feel like the answer was already in place.

What do you think? Do you think that Americans taking away the Native tribes' land was God's will? Do you think it was the obvious course of action? Were there any other ways that Americans could have handled this situation—or was it truly "manifest destiny"?

The United States had started out with the idea that everyone should have freedom. By "everyone" they mostly meant white men, though. Some people worried about this. They started to realize that "everyone" should mean just that—white men as well as black men, Native people, and women. The way people thought was starting to change. But it would take a long time before new laws would be passed.

Americans also had the sense that their freedoms should have no limit. They believed that America should be as big and powerful as possible. But these ideas also led to disagreements. Americans believed in freedom—but they also believed in human rights.

Manifest Destiny justified Americans' settlement of new lands.

EQUAL RIGHTS

America has wonderful beliefs. But Americans haven't always lived up to those beliefs. Still, those beliefs have always been a call to action for Americans. They are reminders that ask us to work hard to treat people more fairly. They remind us to think about what is right. Sometimes, though, it takes years and years for people to change the way they live. It takes years for the reality to catch up with the beliefs.

Can you think of any ways that's still true in America? Are there any groups of people still fighting for the same rights as others? Back in the 1800s, people tried to say they were doing what God wanted, so they didn't have to be fair to everyone. Do people still use that argument today? Do they claim they know what God wants for other groups of people?

These same disagreements came up again and again. Americans' beliefs didn't always seem to work together well. Was America's right to the land more important than the Native people's rights? Whose rights came first? Whites? Or did everyone have equal rights?

These were very hard questions to answer. Americans had different ways of thinking about the problem. Some argued that Manifest Destiny meant they were just doing what God wanted. They relied on "God's will" to explain their actions. Others argued that Africans and Natives weren't really people. If they weren't people, then they didn't need the same rights. Others argued that the United States was making terrible decisions. They saw slavery and the Indian Removal Act as crimes against humanity.

This disagreement continued to shape the United States. The questions about land and human rights were argued over and over. As more settlers moved west, the question would come up again and again. But it would be years before Americans would find the answers.

FIND OUT MORE

In Books

Behrman, Carol H. *Andrew Jackson.* Minneapolis, Minn.: Lerner Publishing Group, 2003.

Evans, Freddi Williams. *The Battle of New Orleans.* Gretna, La.: Pelican Publishing Company, 2005.

Knotts, Bob. *Florida History.* Chicago, Ill.: Heinemann Library, 2008.

Libal, Joyce. *Seminole.* Philadelphia, Pa.: Mason Crest Publishers, 2004.

Raatma, Lucia. *The War of 1812.* Minneapolis, Minn.: Compass Point Books, 2005.

On the Internet

Andrew Jackson
www.u-s-history.com/pages/h154.html
www.classbrain.com/artbiographies/publish/andrew_jackson.shtml

Old Ironsides
www.history.navy.mil/ussconstitution/

Seminole Wars
www.georgiaencyclopedia.org/nge/Article.jsp?path=/HistoryArchaeology/AntebellumEra/Events-7&id=h-842

Shawnee history
www.tolatsga.org/shaw.html

Tecumseh
www.ohiohistorycentral.org/entry.php?rec=373

War of 1812
www.multied.com/1812/Index.html

INDEX

ABOUT THE AUTHOR AND THE CONSULTANT

Michelle Quinby has enjoyed writing ever since she was a little girl. She loves to tell stories that help people understand the world.

Dr. Jack N. Rakove is a professor of history and American studies at Stanford University, where he is director of American studies. The winner of the 1997 Pulitzer Prize in history, Dr. Rakove is the author of *The Unfinished Election of 2000*, *Constitutional Culture and Democratic Rule*, and *James Madison and the Creation of the American Republic*. He is also the president of the Society for the History of the Early American Republic.